Anxiety Sucks!

Emily A. Smith, PhD

authorHOUSE®

AuthorHouse™
1663 Liberty Drive
Bloomington, IN 47403
www.authorhouse.com
Phone: 1-800-839-8640

ISBN: 978-1-4389-8042-3 (sc)

First published by AuthorHouse 4/30/2009

Disclaimer: *The author of this publication makes no warranties, express or implied, with respect to the contents or use of this publication, or any part thereof, and specifically disclaims any express or implied warranties or usefulness for any particular purpose of this publication. The author reserves the right to change or revise this publication, at any time.*

Medical Advice: *The author of this publication is not a medical doctor. Nothing in this publication should be construed as an attempt to offer or render a medical opinion or otherwise engage in the practice of medicine. The medical information provided in this publication is, at best, of a general nature and cannot substitute for the advice of a medical professional. You are urged to consult with a qualified physician regarding personal health questions and conditions. Never disregard professional medical advice or delay in seeking it because of something you have read in this publication.*

Printed in the United States of America
Bloomington, Indiana

This book is printed on acid-free paper.

DEDICATION

This book is dedicated to all of us who have let fear be a front runner in our lives. Life isn't meant to be wasted. It is time to make the change.

Also to my dad, the late James Blair Smith who I miss every single day. And to my Guardian Angel, Anna. Thank you for walking with me and sticking by me, even when I wasn't listening. It must have been excruciating to watch me live my life in fear and self sabotage for so long. Thank you for helping me find a better way and a much happier life. I am truly blessed to know that I am never alone.

DEAR ANXIETY,

I am officially putting you on notice.

Although you have served as a fabulous excuse 'not to' do any sort of real living,

I have to say that that excuse sucks.

It doesn't work for me anymore.

Giving in to you has been the easy way out of life, and I am sick of it.

Because of you, I now know that stepping into my own life and claiming my own power is the only logical choice that I have left.

I don't want to live with regret.

You have served your purpose and now it's time to see you go.

Your days are numbered.

CHAPTER OUTLINE

Introduction

This is not a book that can tell you what way will best help you to make that shift back. It is a support book to let you know that you are not alone in your nightmare and that it does not have to last much longer.

If I would have known – really known – throughout the torture of my own anxiety and panic that I would actually survive it, I would have behaved so much differently. If, during all those years, I would have known that I was not at the brink of death the way I perpetually perceived myself to be, I would have enjoyed myself so much more.

My big fear was dropping dead. I couldn't go anywhere without thinking of who in the room could do CPR, is there a defibrillator handy, and if, God forbid, I did fall out right there on the floor and wasn't actually dying, then would everyone know that I was insane? It was an awful and endless time, full of self-fulfilling prophecies. It absolutely SUCKED. It was lonely and scary and sad, and I lived in it for far too long.

No matter where you are in the anxiety continuum, you do not have to keep this bottled up inside and think that no one could possibly understand the utter crushing chaos of your experience. I'm here. You are not alone. Anxiety does suck, but your life doesn't have to. It's time to make a difference, and it's time to get up and get going. The cycle of wishing for a different outcome and not knowing how to create one is about to be broken, and when it is, where you will be is a place worlds better than where you are right now.

So..."Come along with me...The best is yet to be," says Winnie the Pooh!

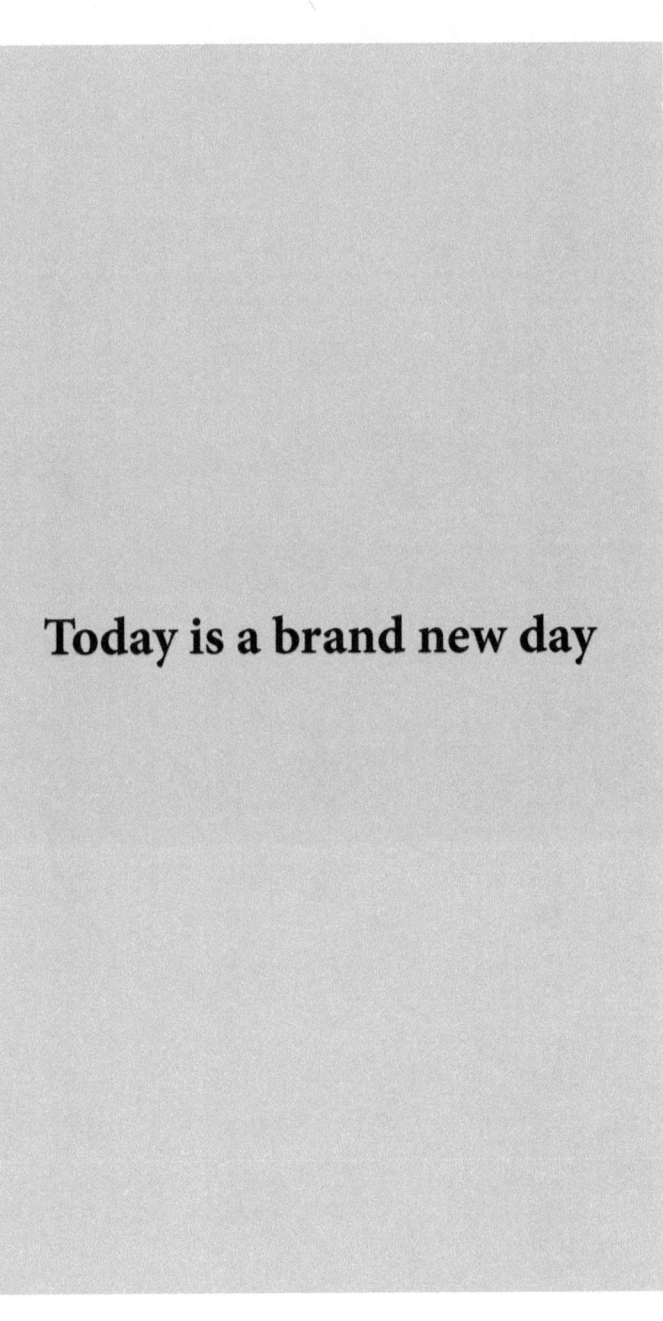

Today is a brand new day

Chapter 1.

ANXIETY REALLY DOES SUCK

Anxiety really does suck, doesn't it? There is not really a better way for me to explain it other than that. It puts you in this holding pattern that is a freaking nightmare to get out of. Unless you have experience with this vicious beast you can't possibly understand just how isolating it is. Haven't you noticed that explaining this condition to a "non anxiety" person makes you sound even crazier than you already feel? It's enough already! I do know how you feel; how lost and hopeless you feel. I have been sitting at the brink of despair more than once with this condition. I have visited all sides of hell with this. Nothing says it better than Anxiety Sucks.

There is more than one type of anxiety. We will look at them in order of severity.

Sometimes when great transitions take place, anxiety comes up. If you are lucky, it is only present during those great transitions and then disappears once you get your life back to level. Even if this is the case, you are now aware that anxiety can become a part of your life, so learn what triggers it and avoid those triggers at all cost. The four biggest contributors to this kind of anxiety are: 1) moving, 2) the death of a friend or member of your family, 3) a divorce, and 4) changing jobs or losing a job. If you are human and these things are happening in your life, how can you not have anxiety? If this paragraph describes where you are right now, give yourself a little slack and gather some support.

Social Anxiety Disorder is the most common emotional disorder. A person with this condition is intensely afraid of making mistakes or being humiliated in social situations. Commonly they are afraid of specific situations such as speaking in public coupled with other social situations. They have a distorted vision, false beliefs about social situations and may create negative opinions about others. People with this condition commonly experience 'anticipatory anxiety' fearing upcoming events for weeks or even months. Often they let their fear make them avoid social situations all together. It is more common in women.

Now, some people have what's called a GAD (Generalized Anxiety Disorder) diagnosis. This is an emotional disorder, not a mental illness, and so does not require lifelong medication. In some cases, it doesn't require any medication at all. In other cases, it would be wise to be open to it.

Panic disorder is anxiety amplified to the point of full blown and frequent attacks. You can call them panic attacks or anxiety attacks – they are the same thing.

Next we move to OCD (Obsessive Compulsive Disorder) which I think of as anxiety exploded. When people have OCD they do certain repetitive rituals before leaving the house, going to bed, or leaving any space or situation in order to ensure that they do not have a panic attack or have discord or upset in their day. The rituals are vitally important to them. OCD is a more serious condition and generally requires medical intervention.

Agoraphobia is anxiety that has taken over completely. This is when the anxiety has gotten so out of control that you do not even want to leave the house. You live in constant fear and it eats you alive. Once this hits, medical intervention is a must.

If you suspect any of these pertain to you then self-diagnosis is not a good idea. Go see a doctor whom you trust and feel comfortable with.

In my experience, every doctor I saw was very quick to prescribe medication. I have conflicting opinions about this. On the one hand, knowing that some doctors get a percentage back from the pharmaceutical companies for each prescription for their medications makes me very suspicious of what the doctors prescribe and how quickly they prescribe them. I have some serious issues with this. On the other hand, I think that sometimes they see better than we do how much better we would feel if we were taking the right medication. It is a contradiction to me and something that led me to quite a few professionals before I found the one that I felt safe with. It turned out to be my primary doctor whom I felt the most comfortable with rather than a psychiatrist, but that was just my own experience.

I will also tell you that the first time that I did try a prescription medication was from a psychiatrist from my insurance provider and the drug was not one that I knew anything about. He said it was their most gentle prescription and one he would give to 80 year old women. He also said that the prescription that I had researched and was interested in was not available on their list of prescriptions from the insurance company. In order for me to be able to try that prescription I would have to go through at least four other types from their list. Keep in mind, you have to be on these drugs for four to six weeks before you can deem them the right or wrong pill. So, when he told me about the gentle one, I gave it a try. I was very afraid of taking it, and rightfully so. I took a fourth of the pill one time and it made me feel like I was in a coma. I was so sedated that I couldn't get out of bed the entire next day (I had taken that pill at night). I called the doctor the next day and told him it felt like someone stuck me in a tunnel and made me smoke an entire bag of weed and that I hated it. I never did take it again. That one day was enough to know that this was not for me.

It took me years to even consider trying anything ever again and I only did because I was so far down that I just couldn't get myself back up on my own anymore. Even today as I sit and write this I decided to try a product that an anxiety center recommended for nutritional support. I can actually hear my heart beating in high definition in my head. It does not feel good. I hate taking pills. I know you do, too. Sometimes they are worth taking the leap of faith for and sometimes they just make things worse. If you do begin a medicinal regimen as prescribed by your doctor, know that if you feel worse, it does generally not get better. It is not the right prescription for you. Of course your body will have to adjust to any medication, but symptoms should be slight and you should be able to feel a positive difference even before the full six weeks have happened.

I had a friend go to the doctor and get on something that made him so much worse. He kept taking it though, because he knew that it took six weeks to really decide if it helped or not. He was a completely different person and in the worst ways possible. Then he gave the medication that I have been on a try and he has become so much more clear in mind! He is happy and thinks it's coincidental that he feels better. He actually doesn't think the medication made that much of a difference, just that his life got better right around the same time. He is still on it, but he really feels only positive effects and nothing negative. That is what any medication should be doing for you, in my humble opinion. When I look into the mirror I see something in my eyes that I thought died a long time ago. It is subtle, but it is tremendously helpful for me. Now that I've been on this medication for a year and a half, I've come down to almost nothing and still feel great. I never even took the lowest adult dose in this whole time either. It was just enough to get me back in charge of my life. This does not in anyway mean that I want you to get on medication. I just want you to realize that being afraid of taking things may or may not be your best bet. I also want you to know that I can certainly understand and appreciate your hesitation about taking anything.

My advice on this subject is to be open, be smart, do your research, and do not do anything that does not resonate within you as a real solution to your suffering. Realize that you do know your body better than any doctor and trust that. Don't let anybody make you feel stupid, silly, or otherwise not in charge of your own feelings or symptoms. There are more people going to the doctors complaining of something being 'off' and being sent home feeling like they are crazy than ever before. Trust what you feel and what your body is telling you about your well-being.

Anxiety is lonely. It's not like we announce out loud our weird and seemingly senseless symptoms. We are not screaming that our face or lips are numb and that our breath is short. We aren't saying that all of a sudden it's hard to swallow, that something is wrong with our gag reflex. Somehow little things in our bodies just stop working normally. We become keenly aware of these little abnormalities, and before we know it... BOOM! We are now surpassing anxiety and heading straight into PANIC! Now this is when things really get good - when we call 911 or imagine ourselves running out of the office with our hair on fire. This is when the beast has taken full control over our brains and climbs to the top of the mountain to flex its muscles and beat on its chest. The Eagle is dead. The Coyote is alive and laughing.

In Native American traditions each animal represents a sacred medicine. Coyote is the medicine of the mind, the trickster who loves to play mind games with us. Coyote likes to make it much more exciting in there and even leads us to believe wild stories and accusations. The medicine of the Eagle is the medicine of the heart. Eagle can soar high above the earth plane and see the bigger picture. This represents the truth and the truth is always far more simple than the exaggerations that the Coyote represents.

In the world of anxiety, Coyote is the bane of our existence, and we banish the Eagle with our every thought. Imagine a little trickster whispering in our ears all of those little 'what ifs' that we hear when we start to feel anxious. It's exciting to listen to that little beast even though we don't realize we are doing it. The truth that tries to show itself is easily swept away by the tidal wave of our emotions and into the sea of despair.

Once we give in to Coyote, we have entered an emotional crack house of fear and unconsciousness where we are always reaching for the next hit, then reaching with equal fervor for something to bring us back down. It's a freaking nightmare! Sometimes we can actually rationalize our way out of it. Sometimes we can dig our way out by visiting all of the patterns that we create to cause such a massacre. Sometimes it takes some medical intervention to help us get out of it and back on track.

**Today
I am free from fear**

Chapter 2.

HOW'S YOUR BREATHING?

Your breathing is a key indicator of where you are in your anxiety. I can spot anxious persons a mile away just because of the way that they breathe. I see it in the grocery store; I can hear it on the telephone. I can see it, and it's time for me to help you end it.

When anxiety begins showing its ugly self, the breath becomes short and shallow. The shoulders begin to rise up with each breath because you feel like you can't get a full breath in. You know this feeling, I know you know it. You start to get a little bit light headed because the oxygen isn't making its way in. Not even the nostrils are cooperating. The lungs seem to be on exit only. Even when that little breath does make its way in, it provides no relaxation in its exhale. It just gets shorter and shorter and harder to get a handle on.

I even knew some people who had this escalate until they would hyperventilate and pass out – in public, in private, it did not matter where they were. It seemed the only way that they could get their breath back on track was by ejecting themselves from the equation. Take the mind out, let the body handle it, and it will work itself out.

Some things to consider when the breath gets short: the body is amazing at correcting itself. It's a term called homeostasis (which is about balance), and it is the body's natural ability to run at optimum levels. Your body is always trying to achieve homeostasis. Our thoughts screw this up but the body will ultimately win the battle. Even if it takes passing out to pause the painful thoughts that have you hyperventilating in the first place, the body will correct itself. Your body knows better than the Coyote. Keep in mind that anxiety and hypochondria are very tight friends.

Another antidote for the breathing predicament is that old wives' tale about breathing into a paper bag – it actually works. When we breathe, we take in oxygen from the air and then release carbon dioxide. When we get overly hyper we seem to keep pulling in the oxygen, and more oxygen, and even more without releasing much at all. We want to reduce the amount of oxygen coming in so that our brains can calm down and our bodies can get back to homeostasis. So, just a few breaths into that bag will do the trick. You can keep one of the old school lunch bags in your glove box in case you need it while you're in or near your vehicle. You know as well as I do that people with anxiety are control freaks and always need to have a viable exit plan in place. The chances of you not having your car are minimal-so keep a bag there!

There are also some really easy breathing techniques that you can do -- both to start the day off right and to correct whatever is going on in the present that is causing you some upset. Here are some examples:

Full Yogic Breaths

Lie down on your back with your arms down by your sides. When you inhale, bring your arms up over your head until your knuckles touch the surface beneath you. Then when you exhale, bring your arms straight back down to your sides. The arms stay straight the whole time and they move at the same speed as your breath. It's super easy, so soothing, and allows you to use 100% of your lung capacity. It's a perfect way to start and end your day.

Fall Out Breaths

In a seated position, either on the floor or in a chair, start with your arms down by your sides. When you inhale, bring your arms around and up over your head. When you exhale, bring the arms back down, making an audible 'ahhh' sound as you do.

Belly Breathing

Lie down on your back, placing one hand on your chest and one hand on your belly. As you inhale, feel the hand on your belly rise up while the hand on your chest sits still. When we get anxious, the breath stays up high in the chest. What we want is for it to come from the belly. Consciously breathing from the belly will relax your body and calm your mind.

Counting Breaths

This is an easy one and is very helpful. A lot of times when we think to breathe deeply, we think about taking a giant inhale and a little bitty exhale. Reverse that and you have a healthy, relaxing breathing pattern! Inhale for a count of 4 and exhale for a count of 8. In your ordinary breathing, you want the exhale to at least be equal in length to the inhale, but as an exercise it's even better to make the exhale twice as long as the inhale.

Breathe Between Your Legs

It's an old school thing, that when you get nervous or feel faint you put your head down and breathe from there, but it's true! When you are just overwhelmed and need a little help calming down and you don't have your brown paper bag on hand, this is the next best thing. Just tuck your head down below your heart and breathe from there for at least 5-10 breaths. Come up slowly on an inhale, and follow it up with a couple of belly breaths.

<u>Yell!</u>
This may sound funny, but it is so useful in so many aspects! When you yell, your exhale has a huge force behind it, emptying the lungs and detoxifying the body. It also releases a lot of aggression and anxiety. Yell and roar and make funny sounds, and see if you don't feel better after you do. Just try it! Once you do, don't waste the release -- go do something that you deeply enjoy doing!

Final thoughts on breathing:

If you start to feel your breath get off pattern, the very best thing you can do to prevent this from turning into panic is to, rather than obsess about the pattern, get your mind on something else. Go get busy. Change locations. Get up, go to the bathroom, walk outside, think of a funny joke, listen to some music. Jump up and down a little bit and get the heart rate going so it can 'handle' the stress you are putting on it. Distract yourself! It will save you so much aggravation – believe me! It is not easy to do in the beginning, but with some time and effort you will begin to get really good at changing things up and having more fun.

Today
I will laugh uncontrollably!

Chapter 3

WHAT'S NUMB?

This one is a biggie: the strange places that we go numb when we get anxious. Sometimes we aren't even feeling anxious until something numbs up! This symptom is my nemesis. It makes me absolutely crazy. I have yet to totally figure out how to head it off other than eating something sweet.

My major triggers for numbing come from drinking alcohol and from not eating regularly. If I drink any alcohol, especially when I haven't had enough sleep, I am guaranteed to start going numb from the tip of my nose out through my cheeks. I can make it go away with food and thoughts. I have to really just put my stress about it to the side and rationalize my way out of it. I say things like, "I know this is an anxiety response and it's not going to kill me. I won't let it stand in the way of what I am doing right now." Once I say this to myself and let it be true, it goes away soon enough. I still hate it, but this helps me defeat it.

Some people get tingling in their fingers and some in their face. I know people who get it in their eyes (not the twitching that we will get to in the next chapter but actual numbing in the eyes). Commonly, though, numbing happens in the lips.

Many times when I have listened to anxiety programs and group discussions about common symptoms and experiences, I really didn't hear anything about numbing in the face. I remember meeting an old friend and our issues with anxiety came up in conversation. The thing that she said that was like music to my ears was that she had just come up the stairs and her face was numb! It felt liberating in a strange way to know that the symptom which most aggravated me, and made me feel the most isolated, did not just happen to me! Someone out there knew what I was experiencing and felt as nutty as I did because of it! Yippee! I am not alone! And, neither are you!

I went to a Doctor about my face going numb, and all she could give me was a diagnosis of 'hypersensitivity' -- that I was simply hypersensitive to my surroundings. I realize now through my years of working with other people that this has a lot to do with what it means to be an empath. Empath's feel in their own bodies strongly what the person we are with is feeling. If I have my hands on a client, I know from my own body's response where the client hurts and what that hurt feels like. I used to think this was a curse, but now I know it is a blessing.

Regardless of which parts anxiety causes to go numb in us, it is a serious distraction. This is one of the symptoms that I just don't deal well with. I tried drinking electrolyte balancing fluids. I tried drinking more alcohol thinking that it could somehow neutralize it which didn't work. I tried eating a candy bar to up the sugar levels. I tried washing my face, putting thick lotions over it thinking that maybe it just needed a little moisture. The truth is, anxiety needs acceptance and acknowledgment followed by a calm attitude toward it, and it will go away.

I truly believe that people who suffer from both anxiety and depression have a very special gift, and because they do not know how to hone that gift or have spent years suppressing it, they create the distraction of emotional distress. There are so many children who are discouraged to explore their special gifts and insights, and so they try to turn them off.

I have always known that I was different than other people. I didn't know exactly how I was different, I just knew that I was. Through studying my own faith and spirituality I have learned that when we elevate to a higher energetic level to communicate with spirits or angels and such, our face can get red or tingly. Hmmmm. Numbing in the face... Tingly or flushed in the face... How similar are those descriptions? Do you see my point? You have a gift my friend, you are super sensitive and up until this point, you haven't embraced this about yourself. Go internal, and investigate yourself! What is it that you have been running from? What is it that you have been trying to hide? Maybe it is time to figure that part of yourself out, let it come to the surface, and find out how to hone it instead of hiding from it. If this paragraph has a peculiar ring to it for you,

check out Indigos and Crystal Children –
you might just be one of those.

Today
I am free from shame

Chapter 4

WHAT'S TWITCHING?

Don't you just hate it when you are trying to go about your day in a normal way and your eye, your finger or thumb, or some other strange part of you starts twitching uncontrollably? It's so frustrating! What can you do about it? Not anything physically, anyway. Again, this is a mind thing. Distract yourself from thinking about the twitch or any stressful thoughts you are having, and it magically goes away!

See, we think too much...about every-thing! All of these symptoms are just the body's way of telling us to chill out. We don't hear that so we keep going and our bodies say, "Oh yeah? Well, why don't you stop for a second and think about this one then?" It's annoying, believe me, I know.

I used to try to research whatever part of my body was twitching to see what emotion it represented. I was very busy for a long time trying to both understand and undermine this insanity of anxiety. It didn't work. If it was my eye, I would take the holistic approach and wonder, "What is it that I am not seeing?" If it was in my hand I would think, "Okay, is it my right hand or my left? The right side is giving, so if it's in my right hand, am I giving more than I'm getting back? If it's my left, am I having difficulty receiving help or love?" Looking at the relationship between emotions and symptom locations has merit. When you are an anxious person, though, you just take those concepts to the Nth degree, and it keeps eating at you. It's never ending. Until it ends. Until you step out. Again, when the twitching starts up, distract yourself. And, do your best to make the distraction a fun one, not stressful. Getting into an argument in order to take your mind off your crazy body symptoms will only bring on more symptoms.

When the twitching sets in, you set out. Accept it as an anxiety response, understand that that is all it is, and go on your merry way. If someone does that thing that we hate and notices it-and asks the question that makes anxiety go from bad to worse ("Are you okay?"), just ignore it and go play with someone else. Get moving...right now! Put this book down and go play! Come back and visit with me again when you feel up to it. You heard me, go out and play! Take a bath, sing a song, dance around like nobody's watching. It doesn't matter what you do -- just go enjoy it!

Today is all that matters

Chapter 5.

YOU DESERVE TO BE HAPPY

Say what? I deserve to be happy? No, I do not. I am really not as nice as you think I am. Actually, I may be too nice. I bend over backwards for everybody. I can't say no; what will they think of me?

- Of course I can do that for you!
- What? You want me to come over and bake a cake?
- Pick up your kids after I pick up my own?
- Do your laundry?
- Write up a proposal for your business?
- Pick up your dry cleaning?
- Fold your clothes once the laundry is done? make your dinner before I go back home and do that for my own family?

Sure! Of course I can! I can't say no! You might think I'm a jerk if I say no! What you have going on is far more important than what I have going on, I know. Sure, I can help -- just tell me what needs to be done. I don't mind at all. I am not too busy. I work better under pressure anyway. The answer is yes.....

It's time to learn some new words, friends. For starters, repeat after me:

NO. Say it again for effect -- NO.

You are not a bad person if the answer is NO.

NO is sometimes (maybe even often) the right answer to the question.

Now, in my case, because I could not say no, I became the person who was unreliable. I would make all these promises, and then when the time came to do whatever I had promised, I just couldn't deliver. Something always came up. Something was always wrong. I may have had a bad feeling about going places, so I would bail at the last minute, pissing people off, and making me feel much worse than I did to start with. Finally, I have learned to own where I am in the moment.

Now when people ask me to do things I reply with phrases like, "Oh, that sounds like fun...We'll see." That is not a promise. I don't make them anymore. I have created a life that includes not committing myself until the event comes close and I know for sure whether I can do it or not. This may sound flaky to you, but at least I do what I say I will do instead of making commitments I can't keep just because I feel obligated to someone beside myself.

I'm tired of being under other people's command. I am tired of feeling obligated to do anything. I am tired of forcing myself to do things I do not want to do. When I do things out of obligation, I don't enjoy myself and the people around me don't get the person they wanted to spend time with anyway. We already waste so much time giving in to our fearful thoughts and behaviors. I don't want to compound that by making promises I should not have made and can not keep. Life is too short and too precious for that.

Aside from feeling like yes people or push overs, we really have to address the whole deserving issue that so often under-pins anxiety. Anxiety is a major form of self punishment. See, we don't deserve to really be happy. We need to be punished for what we did as a child, as a teenager, a lover, a partner, a parent, or in a past life. It doesn't matter what you did wrong or what you have done since -- you must be punished forever.

People who suffer from anxiety truly do not feel worthy of a life filled with happiness and joy. Why would we? Our ministers tell us to fear the wrath of God and the snares of the Devil. Our parents taught us to fear them and God and whatever other things that they instilled in us to fear within ourselves. Our partners threaten to leave us if we aren't "good" as they define it. Everyone threatens us with something at some point in our lives. It's up to us whether we choose to believe it or not, and judging by the fact that you're reading this book, you took the bait.

That's right -- you took the bait. The bait is a bold lie and a one way ticket to hell, and welcome friends -- you've already arrived. Well, what's the good news? You can forgive yourself, see yourself as the magnificent wonder you really are, and know you are free. Now, when you read the part where I called you a magnificent wonder, if you felt any sort of skepticism or doubt, then we have some work to do.

Do you have any idea how thoroughly self-defeating that kind of thinking is? It's a cage and so often we don't even realize that the whole back wall of the cage is not a wall at all! All we have to do is turn around and walk out. This is the hardest part, but we can do it!

Allowing yourself to just enjoy who you are, where you are, and what you are doing may pull a tiny thread that eventually unravels the whole tapestry of anxiety that's been woven in you. But, we are so afraid to do that – to try to undo what has been done and be happy. Are you thinking that nobody you know is really happy? Are you thinking that happiness is an illusion? That even if it isn't an illusion that you are not capable of it? That you don't deserve it? Maybe other people do, but not you? Right? Well that is just NOT TRUE.

That is just not true my friends. The bravest thing that you could do in this situation is to actually cut the cords that keep you stuck and LET YOURSELF have a little fun. Give it a test run. See if you get hit by a bus on the way back! I don't know why we get so crazy about letting ourselves actually enjoy our own lives, or how we can begin to understand that we are responsible for our own lives. We are responsible for our own happiness!

I don't know about you, but when I was at the height of my anxiety, every time I found myself having fun that little voice inside my head would say something like, "You're having too much fun, so watch out -- you're going down." It was the strangest cycle of self-sabotage! And, it occurred for absolutely no reason whatsoever except that I truly did not believe that I deserved to have a little fun! I didn't deserve to have the good life, or to have a happy day! There is no logic in that anywhere, except that somewhere along the line, I believed the lie and made it a truth that I lived by. One day, though, I found my courage. I defied the lie and let myself have fun anyway. Did I go down? I did not. And, neither will you.

To the rest of the world (or the world that we think everybody else lives in) this seems just crazy, right? This internal battle between dark and light? I always felt that I had a really dark side to me, and if anybody got too close or could see me too well then they would be able to see my dark side, too. The truth is, any fear of being dark or defective or 'evil' is proof that you are not dark at all! If you were, believe me, you wouldn't be worried about it! I know now that I had to battle my own fears and face and embrace my light side, it's purity and it's power in order to help myself and help other people. I truly believe that embracing our light is more difficult than sitting with our darkness.

When I went through my yoga teacher training, we had a swami (a renunciate, holy man) come to the ashram to give us our spiritual name and our mantras. The swami spent some time with us and then went into his room to meditate on us for the night. The following day he met with us one on one and did a beautiful ritual and renamed each of us with our new spiritual names. When it came time for my turn, I was nervous. This man was so clean, so pure, so magical and so kind, what would he think when he saw me and meditated on me and my energy? To my great surprise he named me Nirmala, which means "prostrations to she who is free from all impurity." What?! You see this in ME?! How can you see this in ME?! I think I even questioned him how he could see this in me, and he replied that he knew my name as soon as he laid eyes on me the day before. So, if someone so pure could see something this pure in me, then who was I to decide that he was wrong? It was a little tough to swallow and at the same time such a blessing to receive.

As a healing practitioner, I have seen in all of my clients who were in need or battling a life threatening illness something way down deep that tugs at them and tells them they are fated for a life full of some form of punishment or another. They have accepted their fates with no small degree of sorrow and soldier on. It is so sad to see, especially since it is a bold face lie that they have come to believe and give body and breath to. If you have any faith in God whatsoever then start learning and applying the true message of peace. Let go of the lie. Love and acceptance are truly the only way.

We are standing in quicksand and the only way out is to actually let ourselves out. We have to agree with every fiber of our own beings that we deserve to heal, that we deserve to have a happy life filled with joy and passion. Whatever trauma that you experienced that convinced you that you are just not good enough is over – it is in the past. Accept that it happened, love yourself, and let it go. **And until you do fully let it go, no matter what you do, what medicine you take, how often you meditate, how long you live, or who you go to for healing, a healing will not take place.**

I have this very strange way of preparing myself for any kind of competition or public engagement. I have talked about my method to a client of mine who is a well-known PGA golfer. He thinks my method is really interesting and rather crazy and has wondered what a coach or mental health professional would say about it. I figure that I will share it with you, and if you find wisdom in it feel free to give it a shot.

I competed for years in gymnastics and then cheerleading at the collegiate level, and this is how I managed to keep my nerves in check and kick some butt while I was out there. Before I would step onto a competition floor, I would envision myself going out there and completely bombing it. I would actually picture myself falling or bailing out of a stunt or whatever the worst case would have been. I would make myself believe that it had already happened. Why did I do that? Because any time competitors get off the floor after flubbing because they let their nerves get the best of them they always say, "If I could just go back out there and do it again, I would get it right. Please give me another chance," and so on. So, I put myself through that anguish ahead of time so that I have that second chance before I even get out there, and I refuse to let my fear wreck it for me.

Now, try that logic in your daily life! You already live in the worst of it. You are already standing in the muck. Looking back on your life, or even on the day once it is over, isn't there some part of you that says softly, "If I had known I was going to get through it, I would have enjoyed myself so much more..." Do you really think you will be on your death bed wishing that you would have worked more, stressed more, cared more about money, spent less time with your family, or given in to your fears? NO! At that moment, you may wish to have done things differently, but chances are you find a way to own what you did do, ask for forgiveness if you need to, and be at peace. Why wait until then? NOW is the time for you to make amends. Now is the time to conquer your fears. Now is the time to make peace with yourself. Or, do whatever it is you need to do to stop holding yourself so far back. Why have we made it so difficult to let ourselves feel happy? The key? **Forgiveness**. This pertains only to you and not outside of yourself.

Whatever the original situation that preceded your anxiety, it is time to take them by the reins, come into your grown up self and forgive the part of you that was involved. The other people, they don't need your forgiveness. Not really. Forgiveness outside of yourself does not in any way free you of what you have not let go of, and it will not help you heal. We all carry something way deep down that we punish ourselves for, even if we didn't have the power to resist it. We make ourselves the central character in the story of hardship and sometimes, it is simply not your burden to bear. Forgive yourself. Forgive anyone else too if it helps you feel better. But, be honest about that one. Giving forgiveness outward and not doing the same for yourself, may make you feel like a better person, but it makes no difference in your own recovery. If you are angry or harbor deep resentments, feel it. Be angry! Then be willing to let it go after you come into it and feel it. The hard part from there? Walking away from it and not going back for visits, EVER. What is the ultimate truth in any healing? You have to feel your way through it. It can not be analyzed. It can not be rationalized. You will truly only be able to walk away from it once you have felt your way through it. Straight through the middle my friends. Let it burn, let it hurt. Allow yourself to grieve for as long as you need to grieve. I can promise you that once you truly feel your way through, this will be the time when you can walk away from it forever. Getting to the root cause of something is accomplished through understanding and rationalization. Being in a space where you can *apply* the knowledge of the root cause is only done through the actual experience of it.

Bring it up to yourself by re-visiting whatever has stayed stuck deep down for so long, allow yourself to feel it, grieve from it, let it go and walk away from it. Stop chewing on the bone. It's done. It's over. Why are you stuck in perpetual punishment? If there are other people involved in old pains, you can bet that they are not thinking about it quite like you are. You are the only one left in the chamber of pain. Look around you, is anyone else being chained to the wall? NO! Get out of there and move forward. You have officially done enough self punishment for the next ten lives!

Please, please, please, my friends, forgive yourself for whatever it is that is holding you back. Accept yourself and be willing to make the changes necessary to actually come into your life on this Earth! You still have every opportunity in the world to make a difference. You always have a choice. Even if it seems too difficult to deal with, that is your choice. You can choose to heal. If you want to heal, you have to choose it. You have to feel your way out of all of this. Analyzing it and understanding it is all well and good, but until you feel your way through, nothing changes. If you want to be happy, you have to allow it. And, even more than allowing it, you have to accept that you deserve it.

As my favorite saying goes:

"THE UNIVERSE WILL REARRANGE ITSELF TO ACCOMMODATE YOUR PERCEPTION OF REALITY."

My friend and teacher Tom Blue Wolf says that.

What reality do you really want to be living in?

Here is an activity you can do to practice forgiveness. You don't have to know or say what it is that you want to forgive. Even if it is a specific event that comes to mind, be open to the idea that forgiving yourself is much bigger than any event. Go to a mirror and look into your own eyes. Really look. Turn your head in different directions to catch your eyes from different angles. Study yourself and try to see yourself as deeply and as objectively as you can. Once you have gotten into this groove, say out loud to yourself, "I forgive myself. I forgive myself. I forgive you. I forgive you."

If you feel the need to follow that with a recitation of what you are forgiving yourself for, that's okay. After you have forgiven what you want to forgive, it would be amazing if you could look into those eyes and say aloud to yourself, "I love you. I love myself. I love you!"

If you really dig deeply during this activity, you will cry. Go with it. After you do, you will forever be able to look into the mirror and see yourself with loving eyes. You will be free. You DO deserve your own forgiveness and your own love. So, let it happen. You certainly can't get it from anywhere else, not for real, until you can get it from inside of yourself. I forgive you. I love you. I forgive myself and (you guessed it!) I do love myself! I did that ritual for seven days straight and it wasn't pretty and it wasn't fun...until it was.

Today
I will notice miracles

Chapter 6.

BURY THE DEAD AND THE WHAT IF'S

Convincing yourself that you deserve better things and then continuing to beat yourself up on a regular basis is like kicking anything when it's already down. It makes no sense. It's time to bury what's dead in your life along with the vocabulary that hinders your quest for happiness. It's time to change your language.

Did you know that if you are under hypnosis and someone touches you with their bare finger and tells you that they are burning you, you will actually blister? Do you have any idea at all how powerful your mind is? That your powerful mind is susceptible to even the most subtle of influences? We have to wake up to the ways in which we speak to ourselves.

A good place to start is with the words 'what if' -- words that can escalate your anxiety sky high and send you straight to the emergency room. All it takes is a little 'what if' and all hell breaks loose. You know, you get a little short of breath or go numb or start to twitch or all of the above, and then before you know it you are playing the 'what if' game. "What if I am having a heart attack this time?" "What if I pass out?" "What if I have a disease?" "What if I'm dying?" "What if someone jumps out from the corner and tries to rape me, kidnap me or kill me?" What if's are horrible. Get 'what if' out of your head, get it out of your life, and bury it with the dead. Yes, there are ways to turn 'what if' into a positive, but there are simpler paths to a positive outlook and outcome. For now though, get anything that follows the words 'what if' out of your life.

Next, get rid of 'maybe,' 'trying,' 'sort of,' and 'almost.' Just get rid of them. There is nothing good that comes out of being half way to anywhere. You are already an extremist or you wouldn't know anything about anxiety, so use the extremism to your advantage. Either do it or don't, but don't do any of it half way.

'Maybe' sits in between yes and no. 'Sort of' means you're being half-ass about whatever it is. And, you can do better than 'almost.' Be affirmative and be assertive, whatever you do. I heard a quote the other day that said "if you are ready to make a comeback, you must first attend the funeral for your setback." Throw these words into that urn. This, by the way, is the funeral. You have now officially attended the funeral. Now, let's continue toward your comeback!

When I start to feel the fear rushing around me, I pretend that my mind is a tornado slide. I invite the fear in, put it on the slide, and rather than resist, rationalize or reinforce it, I let it sail right on through, out of my body, and into the ground about six feet under.

It used to not be like that for me. Instead of a tornado slide, my mind was a vault with Velcro inside – whatever fear came up in me stuck. Sometimes, still, when fear finds its way in I feel the heart palpitations come. It's okay. Nothing is stuck. I know this is part of the ride. Instead of fighting it or creating something much worse out of it, I call it 'excitement,' and I go with it. The only difference between excitement and fear is what you decide for it to be. So 'bring it on' my friends. Dare it, even. Ask it to pick up speed. This way it comes and goes much faster. Know that you are strong enough, healthy enough and ready to let it come and go with ease and grace.

So, this is it. Let go of your half-way words and ways of living your life. Be as intentional about healing from half-way as you were about giving in to it. Your intention is extremely powerful -- it would have to be to have kept up the anxiety charade for so long. If only you would channel that intention into something more positive! 'If only' -- that's another term to take out of your life. Let's re-do that sentence with something a little more affirmative, and see how much better it sounds: "Now you can channel your intention into something far more positive in your life." Doesn't that feel better?

What about this one -- "When my anxiety gets better, I'm going to join a gym and lose some weight." Why not say, "I am so happy now that I joined a gym because my mind and my body both feel so much better. And, I look great!" Which one feels better?

Be affirmative in your language. Speak as though the outcome has already arrived, and be thankful for it. And for goodness sakes, please be willing to say something nice about yourself! You are a rock star! You are freaking fabulous!

Today
I am free!

Chapter 7.

LIGHTEN YOUR LOAD

Haven't you felt heavy lugging around the weight of all of your self-loathing? It's exhausting! Imagine yourself walking up a mountain with a back pack on your back. Inside the back pack are stones representing particular life experiences. Some of the stones are past relationships, some are things you did wrong that you never got over. That day in the 8th grade when your teacher announced to the class that you were a "stupid little cheerleader who can't pass math and has to get a tutor" (oh wait, that's one of mine!), the day someone you loved so much dropped dead without warning and the years of pain that followed that loss (oops, me again), and the fear of not ever measuring up. Each significant piece of our lives is attached to one of the rocks, and as we walk through each day we add another stone to our packs. Now, at some point we can't go much further because the burden is too heavy to bear. What to do?

Logic would say, "Hey, unload some of those rocks, will ya?" But, that would be too easy and we are not into easy. We don't know how to take the easy way out of anything. That might imply that we like to do things the hard way, but that is not us either! I don't know about you, but I had traveled a long, long way with those rocks on my back, and I didn't even know they were there. I was not resisting letting go – the idea that I had anything to let go of was completely foreign to me.

I figured it out one night while I was outside meditating under the moon. In my meditation, Spirit showed me exactly what I've been talking about -- an image of myself carrying this huge pack on my back, full of heavy rocks. For the first time, I stopped and unloaded. I actually drew an image of each rock on a piece of paper and inside each rock I wrote a single word for what that rock was about – the names of people, feelings, events. After I wrote on each image, I set that piece of paper on fire and buried the ashes. As I did, I felt the heaviness lift off me, and for the first time I felt free.

Do you remember the movie *What About Bob?* If you haven't seen it and you're dealing with anxiety, you might want to check it out. Bob Wiley (the main character, played by Bill Murray) was a nut and sadly similar to myself! There is a scene in that movie where Richard Dreyfuss (who plays the psychiatrist) gives Bob a prescription for his anxiety and it says, "Take a vacation from your problems."

I can think of no better way to say it to you: take a vacation from your problems. Give yourself a break. You got a little off course, and you got a little lost. It's scary and it's lonely, but you are NOT alone. Neither are you nuts.

I used to love going on vacation because it felt like I was taking a vacation from myself. Now, I just live there permanently! I decided that my favorite day of the week was Saturday, so in my world every day is Saturday! I work because I want to and because I love my clients -- not because I have to! I had to change the way I thought about work to do that. I had to change the way I thought about a lot of things so I could be free. Give yourself a break – change your thinking! Oh, how I used to get so anxious doing something that I love so very much. It *almost* made me run from my own destiny.

It's difficult to give yourself a break because you have such high expectations about every little thing that you do. I know. I remember all too well not being able to just lighten up. I used to call it getting into my "screw it mode." And when I would say 'screw it,' it meant that I was going to make a shift and just float on through something for a while. It was my way of giving myself a time out.

I have a friend who is absolutely type A. When she needs a break she calls herself "Petals." When she is Petals, she is calmer, softer, lighter and more care-free. Petals doesn't come out to play very often, but when she does you can actually feel the change in her energy. It may sound funny, but maybe you can give yourself a special name for when your dominant personality needs to take a back seat for a little bit. If that appeals to you, it doesn't mean that you need to add multiple personality disorder to your list of problems -- it just shows that there are playful and light-hearted ways to lessen your load.

Whatever you can do to lighten your load that does not include substances or self-destruction, be open to it. One of the biggest ways that people with anxiety attempt to cope is through drinking and drugging. We are masters of deception and self-medication. We, of course, do not view our wild escapades as self-medication -- we view them as well-earned times when we can escape our issues. At some point, though, it catches up with us. Trust me from my own experience -- when it catches up, it sucks.

I am serious when I say that we all need better remedies and rituals for relief. We all need better ways of recognizing what is real in us so we will know how to care for ourselves in loving and productive ways. Know what triggers the worst in you, and learn little things to cut that off at the pass. Learn how to let go. Learn ways to have a good time that are healthy, simple, and safe.

Make some new friends if you need to who can enjoy a clean night of good fun. I used to wonder what in the world people actually did on the weekends if they weren't out at the bars. I remember having a conversation with someone standing in a bar and saying, "I will party forever." If people weren't partying, I didn't see how they could possibly be having any fun. I mean, what do they do? Go to the movies, go bowling, what? What do they do with themselves?

As it turns out, it is in no way boring to wake up on a Saturday morning without a hangover and actually have a productive day! Who knew? Better than that, it is actually stimulating to spend my weekends with like-minded people who live healthy, happy lives! And, even better than that, I have found ways to achieve a total body and mental 'high' without any substances whatsoever: yoga, meditation, workshops, dancing, singing, etc. If you don't think those are things you could do or enjoy on your own, there are groups out there for everything!

Not only do I go out of my way to have fun, I can also enjoy an utterly lazy day. I do not feel guilty anymore if I spend a whole day in my pajamas. It's all in the perspective. It is high time that you change yours if you cannot allow yourself whole days here and there to chill out.

Enough is enough. Give yourself a break! You deserve it!

Today
I will get outof my head

Chapter 8.

UNDERSTANDING THE MIND/BRAIN

The mind and the brain are two entirely different entities. The brain is an organ and when it gets out of whack chemically it can't always balance itself. When this is the case, intervention is required. This can be done with medication or herbs, depending on the severity of the imbalance.

If it were another organ that had the issue, you would not hesitate to do what you could to help it get back to good health. I did not understand that for many years. I was so against medication and did everything I could to avoid it -- I felt like having pharmaceutical help would be hypocritical, considering my holistic lifestyle. Some of my refusal was based on my belief that my mind and my brain were the same thing.

I tried counseling, herbs, acupuncture, EMDR (eye movement desensitization reprocessing), soul retrieval, energetic extractions, anxiety programs, acceptance and commitment therapy, psychics, mediums, quantum physics biofeedback, more herbs, vitamins, tinctures, books, programs, yoga, massage, tai chi, reiki and various other healing styles. You name it and seriously, I did it. For over seven years I committed myself to healing from anxiety naturally.

When I started seeing a psychiatrist I asked him if we could alter the chemicals in our brains without medication. He said that, yes, it is entirely possible, but that most people did not have the discipline or the dedication to make this happen. I thought that I would be that one who proved him wrong. And, for a while, doing it my way worked.

Sometimes, though, this kind of effort is not enough to change your brain for the better. Sometimes you are deficient in certain chemicals, and right thinking can't quite counter that deficiency. I just know that despite my best efforts, when life got a whole lot harder to handle, those efforts became ineffective.

I finally caved and gave medication a try, and to my surprise, it helped in ways I had never imagined! I am not saying everybody should take medicine. I just know that if someone could have made me understand that I would feel as good as I felt once I gave it a try, I would not have struggled seven whole years trying to handle it on my own. For me, even though I only took a child's dose of the medication, it made a profound and positive difference in my daily life.

The mind is not the same thing as the brain. The mind is where the ego lives, and it can play some nasty tricks on you. The mind is emotional.

In the yoga training we learned that there is something called samskaras or mind grooves. When we habitually think a thought, and choose to continue to think that thought, we create grooves in our mind, much like driving at a consistent speed in a new car creates grooves in the engine wall.

To change our thought patterns requires a lot of awareness, intention, dedication and patience. It is entirely possible to do, but it is not easy and it will not happen over night.

Buddhists talk about the 'monkey mind,' that restless mind chatter that we know so well. When I am trying to get in a good space, or when I can feel my monkey mind getting more aggressive, I imagine a very heavy box. I gather up my monkey, put it in the box, and close the lid securely. Once I do this, I imagine sliding the box outside of my space.

Had I not done the years of work developing coping mechanisms and cultivating my higher self, I can't really see the outcome being quite as pleasant-medication or not. I put in a whole lot of effort to get better from this condition long before I ever tried any prescription, and I have been committed to the healing during and after medical intervention. I have done many Native American sweat lodges and still do. I also have done two fire walks (yes, walking on hot coals to overcome my own fears, and, yes, it was hot and do not let anybody tell you different!).

I also began to put myself out there in life situations that I always knew I was meant to be a part of but never had been. I began doing public speaking engagements and facing my fears head on. It wasn't easy, and it wasn't necessarily fun either. The rewards, however, have far outweighed the discomfort of my efforts. Perfect example:

I spoke at a local hospital for a cancer support group on alternative healing and finding ways to find comfort within during chemotherapy. As I got there, I became frantic! My speech began to speed and I began to jump inside my head and get lost in it. I was finished with my talk in less than ten minutes, no joke. Then when I was ready to run out and cry at my terrible behavior, someone asked me a question.

As I looked up and looked around the room at these people who are fighting for their lives and were looking to me for any support, I told myself that it was time to get out of my head and offer what is mine to give. And so I did. I backed up and started over. I took a deep breath and started again. This time, I was calm and interested in them and not myself. It ended up being a wonderful afternoon and I felt fantastic!

Now, the old "anxiety riddled" me would have gone out of there and given myself a back lash for my behavior. But, the new me, the more conscious me, gave myself great praise! I got in the elevator, looked at my reflection and said out loud to myself: "You Did It!" No one else cares anywhere near what we do about silly mishaps that we may have. We are human and we are allowed to mess up. Even greater than that, we are allowed to back up and punt. No one is harder on us than we are, and that needs to change.

I have become my greatest supporter instead of my biggest critic. I congratulate myself on the little things that may go unnoticed by anybody else. I have a new scale upon which to measure myself, and it has nothing to do with other people. I also get excited over the little things, which does make life so much more fun!

Personally I feel like I have come back from the dead, and I have a lot of living to do! I have spent so much time living in fear, and that isn't living at all. Now that I know how to let my fear go, what is left in my life is joy, and that is such a surprise! For me, with the help of my small dose of medication, I can really understand that the brain really is its own organ and when it is a healthy one, life can be fun again. Now I can participate in my own life. Do I wish that I could have done this years ago? Of course I do. But, I am not going to beat myself up for that, because that is going backward. Anxiety is going backward. Guilt is going backward.

Shame is going backward. Now that I can remember what fun and freedom feel like, I don't have to go backward anymore.

I will say it again loudly: ANXIETY SUCKS. It's a condition I truly wish I could rid the world of, one beautiful person at a time. To watch old videos of myself when I would breathe so shallow and short, when my eyes looked glazed over because I was living in a nightmare of my own making -- it makes me want to cry. When I look at other people now who are feeling this way, it makes me want to jump on them, shake them, and say, "STOP!!! There is a way out!" Your way out may have nothing at all to do with medicine, or herbs, or fire walks, or look like my way out at all. Each person has their own triggers and their own releases. They are there -- it is up to us to find out what they are.

Mostly, though, no matter what your triggers or releases may be, the key is to give yourself permission to heal. You have to give yourself permission not only to heal, but also to have fun. You have been the gatekeeper to your emotions and up to this point, you have not served yourself so well. Step aside and let the true gatekeepers take over -- your angels, your spirit guides, your

God. Whatever you call them, they have much higher allowances for our happiness than we do. They are good at what they do – so much better than we are!

The truth is, the celestial beings actually want you to be happy and to enjoy your life. It's hard to believe, I know, but it is true. Please, for your kids' sake, for your partner's sake, for your animals' sake, for your soul's sake -- let yourself enjoy your life in the way that we are all meant to. Rearrange your own internal rules so you can be the light, love and laughter you are meant to be. Your greatest joy is waiting for you right now – go get it with the same intensity and the same sense of inevitability with which you've held on to your anxiety. I promise you will be so very glad you did.

**Today
I will wake up to my life!**

Chapter 9.

AREN'T YOU TIRED YET?

The choice is ALWAYS yours. And, there is always an opportunity to choose again if what you chose this time didn't work out. Happiness is a choice. Shame, fear, and guilt are choices, too. Punishing yourself and living in shame, fear, or guilt is such a lousy way of living and it is your choice to buy into it or not. By deciding you deserve to be punished, or feel guilty, is like slapping God in the face. It's taking control in a way that is so unhealthy. Contrary to your popular belief, you are not in charge!

If you are one of those people who really does feel that you do not deserve the happiness and freedom that Spirit offers you, imagine the person whom you think is the most wonderful person you know. They can be infants with purity and light, they can be elderly with wisdom and humor. They can be your best friend, your sibling, your mentor-it really doesn't matter who it is, just see them in your mind. Now think of all the wonderful qualities about that person that you admire. Close your eyes, go on, don't skip this part. Really think about this and feel it. You know that you have achieved this step if you find yourself smiling right now. Now, an absolute law of the Universe is that there is NO way that you would be able to see any of those qualities if you did not posses them yourself! HA! What do you think of that! You already are what you so desperately want to be! You couldn't see them if they were not already present in you! I had to say it again for dramatic effect. Do you see it yet? You are fabulous, too!

Do you see the logic in all of this? Step into your own life! Claim your own power! It's time to face up to the fact that living out loud is far more daring than living as if you were dead. To step into your own life and claim your own power is the road less traveled.

You think that you are alone in this? Not even close! Everyone is neurotic! Everyone is dealing with something, even if you don't know them well enough to see it. Being human is complicated! It's also a gift. It's not a permanent gift, though, so please -- get out there and get into your life! Take the leap, and the net really will appear. You are NOT ALONE, you NEVER were, and you NEVER will be. Your best life is waiting for you right now...when are you going to test out that theory? If we could use our tenacity and our commitment toward something good, we could see this. Take off those black grim glasses and put on some with rose colors! Imagine the song "I can see clearly now, the rain is gone" playing in the background as you read this!

Now, having read what you've read so far, don't you feel like celebrating? Please say YES, and mean it! You are in charge of how you handle the difficult stuff. You are in charge of making sure you laugh more than you cry. You might still feel fear, but you are in charge of whether or not you give in to it. Admit out loud that you are afraid, and then all of a sudden fear loses its hold on you.

Anxiety is so self-absorbing that it feels like it can only be all about me. We get so stuck in our own heads that there really is no room for anyone else! That looks so pathetic on paper, but you know it's true. It sucks, but it is true. When you are in emotional chaos, you have no room in your head or your heart for anyone but you. That darn coyote is screaming in your ear, and there is nothing for you to feel except fear and frustration.

When you realize that it's not all about you, you won't be so afraid anymore. When you are convinced that the world is out to get you, repeat after me: "It's not all about me." Or, as I really like to think of it, I say to myself in my most slang voice "You ain't all that!"

My friend is a personal trainer and one morning he was training this woman who became absolutely obsessed because she didn't put on her makeup that morning. As the club became more crowded than usual, she could not focus on her work out, she could only focus on the thought that everyone was staring at her. My friend said to me, "all I wanted to say to her is, girl, you ain't all that!" For some reason, it stuck with me and whenever I feel like the world is closing in on me and my anxiety is becoming consuming I say that to myself in a joking manner to bring me back down to reality. "You ain't all that!"

Of course, you are truly all that and more, but not in this particular situation.

It's not all about you. On the other hand, know that it includes you. You are here and you are real. You are an invaluable source of love and light. You are a very particular and sacred part of this planet. Without you, nothing would be the same. Now make something of your special self that you can celebrate. No more wasting life.

It is the time my beautiful friends – time to jump in and get dirty and roll around like a pig in mud. It's time to play and laugh and cry, and scream at the top of your lungs. It is time for you to live your life in a new way. Make new choices. Face your fears -- they are nowhere near as painful as you have made them out to be. Embrace the hard stuff. Enjoy the easy stuff. Crank up the music, and dance! Put on Gloria Gaynor's *I Will Survive* and know that you already have! You can tell that I live by music. It would be awesome if this book busted out with my playlist as you are reading it...something to invent for the future! Be thankful. Be gentle with yourself. Be well.

**Today
I will pay it forward!**

Chapter 10

THE CELEBRATION!

You are allowed to celebrate! Take time to enjoy your breath. Look up at the moon every night. Take notice of the little things -- they are all miracles, and they are wasted if they go unnoticed. Wake up to your life! No one will do it for you, and no one else can. It is your decision: to really live, or to just walk among the living as if you were dead. Giving in to fear is a fate worse than death itself. Constantly punishing yourself is the same thing. If you are reading this, then guess what? You are still alive! That means you still have the choice to change your patterns, and give yourself permission to say, "I deserve to have some fun, and darn it, I'm going to. Right now!" Change up the rules, change up the expectations and go be free! You are allowed to celebrate, my brothers and sisters! It is time to free yourself from your burdens and fears and jump into a new way of being!

Those who only know you as the anxious one may not like the new you. Certain people will not want the changes that will come with your new-found happiness. If your relationship with that person is really important, go to counseling together, or whatever, but please don't let his or her resistance impede your progress.

All you can hope for with your partner, family and friends is that they are strong enough to love you through this and strong enough within themselves that they can handle not being 'needed' the way they used to be. Coming up to higher ground unsettles things, but honey, it is something to behold! It's a beautiful place, and you belong there. Don't let anything or anyone take that away from you.

Coming into a place where you can face your fears and then throw them out is so liberating, and I can only hope that you are already beginning to feel that new feeling coming up inside you as you read this! You deserve to be happy! You deserve to be healthy! You deserve to be FREE from fear, burdens, guilt, shame and whatever other crappy feelings which have been following you around. NO MORE, NO MORE, NO MORE! You DESERVE to be FREE and with a little work, YOU CAN BE!!!

Now, go do something wonderful for yourself. Throw yourself a party! Take yourself out for a meal, for a massage, for whatever you do that feels like a treat, go do it! I get being reasonable with your money, but you don't have to live like a pauper. Use the good china! Burn those beautiful candles! Open up the presents you are given and use them yourself instead of giving them to someone else! Enjoy what you have! Enjoy who you are! Enjoy everything!

Changing is your choice. But if you weren't really willing to change, would you have found or bought this book? Imagine that you've been sitting in an old building full of smoke that has been on fire for years. I am the fire fighter woman who has come to rescue you and bring you out of that burning building. I carry you out, clean you off, give you a change of clothes, and send you back out into the world. The smoke has cleared, and you can see what's left of the building you've been trapped in for so long. What are you going to do now? There is a whole big world out there, and you are part of it! Go be wonderful! Breathe! Become!

It is time to make a difference. You didn't go through this for nothing. Pay it forward. Be the changes you want the people around you to make. Offer help and support to those that are still standing where you were for so long.

I am proud of you, and I am excited for you! Now, stop reading this book, and get your butt out there!

You heard me, get out there!

What are you waiting for?

Don't make me come up there!

Go on, get going!

And, wherever you are headed,

CELEBRATE WHO YOU ARE!

Peace-

Today
I am the inspiration

Acknowledgments

Written by Emily A. Smith, PhD
Edited by Ashli Callaway, MDiv
Final Proof Reading by Frank Blau
Head Shot by Fran Cooper

I have many to thank who helped me heal when I was at my worst (whom I will mention by name) and those who helped me to pay it forward while you stood by me (you know who you are). I apologize if I have left anyone off the list.

Arthur Fretwell, Bobby McCall, Ashli Callaway, Pamela Bellamy, Tom Blue Wolf, Yellow Horse Man, Dr. Du, Kris Bush, Michael Colley, Carola Kauffhold, Mikhail Raznobriadsev, Dattatreya, Heather Hale, Natasha and Darryl Jones, Joanna Sole, Sherry Leethem, Art Webster, The Atlanta School of Massage, Christi Dickey, Buffy Smith, Jan Godfrey, Stuart Pflug, Valorie Grosso, Lee Zajack, Thom Rutledge, Don Miller, Laura Ward, Rosalee Sirgany, Anthony DeMello's teachings and writings, Dr. David

M. Reingold, Father Hennessey, Father Tom Francis, Neale Donald Walsh, Lucinda Bassett, and my entire family and friends as well as my support group from the spirit realm -- you have certainly had your work cut out for you!

Most of all, thank you to my clients and friends who have found me over the years to be a support to you in your times of personal crises. And to all of you whom I have yet to meet who need support. I look forward to being a part of your recovery and your journey into the next and much better part of your life. Sometimes you stay down until you just have to get tired of being down. No matter how long it takes, you will get better. And it does only get better from here.

Namaste.

ABOUT EMILY A. SMITH

Emily holds a BS in Exercise Science and Wellness with a minor in Nutrition from Jacksonville State University. She has a Masters of Philosophy and a PhD specializing in Comparative Religion from the University of Sedona. She is a graduate of the Atlanta School of Massage in Clinical and Neuromuscular Massage Therapy as well as a Dr. Vodder Manual Lymph Drainage Therapist. She is a Universal Yoga Teacher in Sivananda Yoga, as well as a Usui and Karuna Ki Reiki Master. She is also a Seven Rays practitioner, working directly with the Ascended Masters.

She is the author of:
Awaken: To Expanded Consciousness
Stretch Therapy: A Comprehensive Guide to Basic Stretching
Stretch Therapy II: A Comprehensive Guide to Basic Assisted Stretching
Come Into Being: Guided Meditation CD
Create Your Day/Celebrate Your Night
Anxiety AM/PM Meditation CD

Emily's mission statement is: To help facilitate the healing and retraining of the body's ability to heal itself.
Go to www.spiritwavehealing for more information, to schedule workshops, order products or to contact Emily.